Stoning Demons

Complex PTSD Recovery Workbook

*****

By Kimberly Callis

SMASHWORDS EDITION

ISBN :9781511647564

*****

Table of Contents

Purpose of this Workbook

This workbook is focused on Complex Post-Traumatic Stress Disorder (C-PTSD) as it relates to developmental trauma. The workbook supports the Stoning Demons series of books and uses recovery approaches outlined in Book 5, Recovery and Therapy for Complex PTSD.

The purpose of the workbook is to give examples of the methods and tools that I used as an informed patient through the course of my recovery from Complex PTSD.

About the Stoning Demons Series

In this series, I will share some of the core research I have discovered on CPTSD, developmental trauma and marijuana-supported therapy. I have provided references to materials that I have found helpful in better understanding my own condition.

The material also covers the related physical health impacts that developmental trauma and early life PTSD can have. I share my history, which involves chronic disease and disability, all likely stemming from childhood abuse and neglect. There are ample resources to support this conclusion, which I also share.

Throughout the series, I openly discuss my use of marijuana as self-medication and support for my recovery process and maintenance. I have made it my personal ambition to address this topic openly, clearly, without shame or judgment, in ways that will open the doors for better understanding and healing.

This work emphasizes the need for a holistic approach to recovery and looks at the effects of stress, nutrition and toxins. Once I made the connection between wellness and mental health, I started to find the stability I needed to address the psychological and developmental effects of my condition.

I find it encouraging that more information is becoming available and that more people are finding understanding, help, and hope. The challenge is that not all of this information is presented in clear, unbiased, readable terms and there are very few resources that offer a holistic view.

Let me emphasize that I am not a medical doctor or psychology professional. I am a survivor, an informed patient. My perspective comes from personal experience, personal research and personal analysis. I do not claim any academic expertise, nor do I intend this book to serve as professional advice. I do hope that the reader will find inspiration for their own healing process and references that are useful.

My Story

Use this section to tell your history, your experience and your feelings about how your life was affected. You may want to add to this or revise it as you use this workbook. It will help to re-read it regularly as you work on your recovery. It will help you uncover more aspects of your experience that are relevant and will help you find a way to understand it, analyze is and accept it.

My Childhood

My Adult Life, So Far

What It All Means To Me

Trauma Inventory

Use this section to make a list of traumatic events and situations you have experienced in your life. Classify these by the type of event you have dealt with so that you can better understand the effect that may have had. This will help guide your recovery and management plan.

Doing this may be confronting, so go at your own pace. If you feel triggered by the exercise, stop and come back to it later when you feel you are ready.

Traumatic Event	Contributing Situation	Type of Trauma	People Involved
Emotional abuse	*Parent's divorce, father's alcoholism*	⊗ *Traumatic Injury/Illness* ⊗ *Traumatic Grief* ⊗ *Traumatic Attachment* ⊗ *Traumatic Sexualization* ⊗ *Traumatic Identity Formation*	*Father*

Traumatic Event	Contributing Situation	Type of Trauma	People Involved
Emotional abuse	*Parent's divorce, father's alcoholism*	⊗ *Traumatic Injury/Illness* ⊗ *Traumatic Grief* ⊗ *Traumatic Attachment* ⊗ *Traumatic Sexualization* ⊗ *Traumatic Identity Formation*	*Father*

Symptom Inventory

Use this section to make a list of symptoms you experience with your Complex PTSD. This exercise will help you do a simple analysis of the feelings, triggers, thoughts that come with them and determine how you can best respond.

Symptom	When Do I Experience It?	How Do I Experience It?	Typical Situation	Best Response
		Physically		
		Emotionally		

Symptom	When Do I Experience It?	How Do I Experience It?	Typical Situation	Best Response
		Physically		
		Emotionally		

Symptom	When Do I Experience It?	How Do I Experience It?	Typical Situation	Best Response
		Physically		
		Emotionally		

Symptom	When Do I Experience It?	How Do I Experience It?		Typical Situation	Best Response
		Physically			
		Emotionally			

Symptom	When Do I Experience It?	How Do I Experience It?		Typical Situation	Best Response
		Physically			
		Emotionally			

Symptom	When Do I Experience It?	How Do I Experience It?		Typical Situation	Best Response
		Physically			
		Emotionally			

Symptom	When Do I Experience It?	How Do I Experience It?		Typical Situation	Best Response
		Physically			
		Emotionally			

Symptom	When Do I Experience It?	How Do I Experience It?		Typical Situation	Best Response
		Physically			
		Emotionally			

Symptom	When Do I Experience It?	How Do I Experience It?		Typical Situation	Best Response
		Physically			
		Emotionally			

Trigger Inventory

Use this section to make a list of situations, events, smells, places, people, and words, anything that causes a flashback or intrusive dreams. This will help you find coping mechanisms, therapies and recovery approaches to help reduce the impact of triggers.

Trigger	What Happens Mentally?	What Happens Emotionally?	What Happens Physically?	Best Response

Trigger	What Happens Mentally?	What Happens Emotionally?	What Happens Physically?	Best Response

Symptom Journal

I keep a symptom journal, mostly updating it when I actually feel bad. This really helped when I was trying to understand what was going on with experiencing physical symptoms of CPTSD without the typical mental or emotional symptoms.

Date & Time	Symptoms	Situation	Thoughts	Feelings
Example	Anxiety, butterflies in my stomach, sense of doom	I have an appointment to get my hair done	Numb, not really thinking	Nervous, scared to see people, don't want to go outside
		Physical Health		Life Stress
What else is going on?	Did not eat breakfast Tired from not sleeping last night		Busy getting everything done to go out of town	

Date & Time	Symptoms	Situation	Thoughts	Feelings
		Physical Health		Life Stress

Date & Time	Symptoms	Situation	Thoughts	Feelings
		Physical Health		Life Stress

Date & Time	Symptoms	Situation	Thoughts	Feelings
	Physical Health		**Life Stress**	

Date & Time	Symptoms	Situation	Thoughts	Feelings
	Physical Health		**Life Stress**	

Date & Time	Symptoms	Situation	Thoughts	Feelings
	Physical Health		**Life Stress**	

Date & Time	Symptoms	Situation	Thoughts	Feelings

	Physical Health		Life Stress	

Date & Time	Symptoms	Situation	Thoughts	Feelings

	Physical Health		Life Stress	

Date & Time	Symptoms	Situation	Thoughts	Feelings

	Physical Health		Life Stress	

Intrusive Thoughts Journal

Use this journal to record intrusive thoughts. Keeping track will help you understand how they are contributing to bad thoughts, feelings and other symptoms.

Date & Time	Intrusive Thoughts	Situation	Thoughts	Feelings
Example	Called myself stupid, felt stupid all day	What was going on that made me think these things?	What voice am I using?	What affect do these thoughts have on me?

Date & Time	Intrusive Thoughts	Situation	Thoughts	Feelings
Example	*Called myself stupid, felt stupid all day*	*What was going on that made me think these things?*	*What voice am I using?*	*What affect do these thoughts have on me?*

Flashback/Dream Journal

Use this section to keep a journal or list of all of the flashbacks experienced. This list can be associated with trauma memories. I found it helpful for understanding what I was remembering and how it bothered me.

Flashbacks are a bit different from intrusive thoughts. They are like reliving or re-experiencing. Try to capture as many details about the flashback as you can... who is involved, where you were, what was going on, how you felt, what the real conflict or fear might be...

Date & Time	Flashback/Dream	Reactions	Feelings
	Are there triggers that cause the flashbacks?	Can I reframe my response to them?	

Date & Time	Flashback/Dream	Reactions	Feelings
	Are there triggers that cause the flashbacks?	Can I reframe my response to them?	

Date & Time	Flashback/Dream	Reactions	Feelings
	Are there triggers that cause the flashbacks?	Can I reframe my response to them?	

Date & Time	Flashback/Dream	Reactions	Feelings
	Are there triggers that cause the flashbacks?	Can I reframe my response to them?	

Date & Time	Flashback/Dream	Reactions	Feelings
	Are there triggers that cause the flashbacks?	Can I reframe my response to them?	

Date & Time	Flashback/Dream	Reactions	Feelings
	Are there triggers that cause the flashbacks?	Can I reframe my response to them?	

Date & Time	Flashback/Dream		Reactions	Feelings
	Are there triggers that cause the flashbacks?		Can I reframe my response to them?	

Date & Time	Flashback/Dream		Reactions	Feelings
	Are there triggers that cause the flashbacks?		Can I reframe my response to them?	

Recovery Plan

Recovery Goals	
What Do I Want to Achieve?	How Will I Stick to My Goals?

Stabilization Plan	
What Are My Most Critical Issues? Anxiety, depression, panic attacks	What Do I Need to Maintain Stability?

Professional Support	
Doctor	
Therapist	
Crisis Center	
Group	

Personal Support Network	

Primary Trauma Work	
What Do I Need to Do?	
What Resources Do I Need?	
What Will I Gain From This?	
How Long Will It Take?	

Primary Role Work	
What Do I Need to Do?	
What Resources Do I Need?	
What Will I Gain From This?	
How Long Will It Take?	

Secondary Trauma Work	
What Do I Need to Do?	
What Resources Do I Need?	
What Will I Gain From This?	
How Long Will It Take?	

Narrative Therapy	
What Do I Need to Do?	
What Resources Do I Need?	
What Will I Gain From This?	
How Long Will It Take?	

Medical Therapy	
What Do I Need to Do?	
What Resources Do I Need?	
What Will I Gain From This?	
How Long Will It Take?	

Skill Development Plan	
What Do I Need to Do?	
What Resources Do I Need?	
What Will I Gain From This?	
How Long Will It Take?	

Nutritional Plan	
What Do I Need to Do?	
What Resources Do I Need?	
What Will I Gain From This?	
How Long Will It Take?	

Exercise Plan	
What Do I Need to Do?	
What Resources Do I Need?	
What Will I Gain From This?	
How Long Will It Take?	

Stress Management Plan	
What Do I Need to Do?	
What Resources Do I Need?	
What Will I Gain From This?	
How Long Will It Take?	

Personal Growth Plan	
What Do I Need to Do?	
What Resources Do I Need?	
What Will I Gain From This?	
How Long Will It Take?	

Primary Trauma Work

Primary Role Work

Secondary Trauma Work

Recognizing Strengths

Acceptance

Personal Goals

Growth Inventory

Capturing an inventory of ways that I have grown and thrived, even just coped, helped me see that I am not just the sum of my experiences... I am all of the strengths I gained and gave to get through them. I think this exercise helped me find some anchors for self-love and compassion that I needed.

How I Have Grown?	What Have I Gained?	How Do I Feel About It?

Management Plan

Action	Frequency	Benefit	Motivation
Stress Management Medication Nutrition Exercise			

Crisis Plan

Use this section to outline IN BOLD LETTERS AND CLEAR TERMS what to do in a PTSD crisis. This page will be used by you and your personal support network to help in difficult times when your symptoms are hard to manage on your own.

Crisis Situation	What To Do	Critical Details
FEELING DEPRESSED	Call my sister	555 555 5555

www.ingramcontent.com/pod-product-compliance
Lightning Source LLC
Chambersburg PA
CBHW041523280526
45792CB00004B/1360